LANKY SPOKE

CW00434558

The Legendary Comical Tongue-in-Che~~ ~~~~ ~~ ~~~ ~~~~~
Dialect

By Dave Dutton

(Author of Lanky Panky and Lancashire Laughter and Tears also
available on Kindle and in print)

www.davedutton.co.uk

T'Contents

Foreword

A Tripe Curtain has descended across Britain, sithee - Winston Churchill (1874-1965)

Ey up theer! So tha's tekken it inter thi yed ter cum'n hiya sken ut Lankysher hasta? Well wur reet gradely fain ter see thi!

Well hello there! So you have decided to have a look at Lancashire have you? Well, we are extremely pleased to see you!

Thus may the ears of the visitor to Lancashire be assailed by this unfamiliar tongue. For the dialect still flourishes in Lancashire and the visitor will encounter a bewildering array of words and phrases that to him or her will be in a language as foreign as Serbo-Croat or Russian. The discomfiture of the visitor is purely unintentional as that is how people talk in Lancashire and is as undeniable a fact of life as the French speaking French and the Germans speaking German. Therefore, to help minimise the bewilderment, I have compiled this phrase book which, I hope, will prove indispensable to the visitor as he attempts to communicate with the native in his natural habitat. The bureaucrats may have mucked about with the boundaries of the old county, but for most people Lancashire will always be where good old 'Lanky' is spokken. The visitor will encounter dialect spoken in tap rooms, schoolyards, factories, pits, park benches, rugby league and football matches, youth clubs, cafés, street corners and the hearthside: in fact, here, there and everywhere. The visitor will be amazed at the variety of beautiful scenery within a *'cockstride'* of some of the country's most industrialised areas but wherever the visitor goes, the dialect will always be there: and why shouldn't it be?

The dialect enriches the quality of life: it is what makes Us different from Them; it expresses true emotions in warm human terms, that otherwise would sound forced and stilted; it is a badge which identifies the wearer; it betokens roots and stability in a changing age; it is the cohesive voice of a people; it rings true; it is reassuring; it is unique; it is peculiar; it fits like a coat; it is gradely; it is tough; it is tender; It is beautiful; it is worth preserving; it survives. Long Live Lanky! - *David Dutton, Lancashire.* *

* I wrote that foreword in 1978 when Lancashire was a different place both culturally, socially and economically. Some of the dialect

has faded along with memories of the mills and mines which made up a major part of the Lanky landscape and the older workers who spoke the dialect strongly. It still exists though in pockets of resistance and indeed seems to have had some sort of renaissance through groups like the Lancashire Hotpots who play major music festivals and have a young following who love their Lanky humour. Humour is what it's all about. I'm not claiming everyone in Lancashire speaks like this and dialect also varies within the county. A moggy can be a mouse in some parts and a cat in others! *(As discussed in* **Lanky Panky!** *My 2nd book in the series which is also available as an ebook and in print).*

Take this book for what it is then: a comical (I hope!) tongue-in-cheek guide to the Lanky lingo from a mon who is proud to be from the county of the Red Rose. Spread the word. Educate the unenlightened. Tell yer family and friends as well. And may the Good Lord never drop a clog on yer yed!

Reetoh.

Let's start with…

The Lanky Definite Article

There is no Lanky definite article. Merely substitute a small half-strangled explosion of air from the back of the throat. Therefore, 'down the colliery' 'becomes 'deawn pit'. Master this and you have mastered the first basic rule of speaking Lanky.

Basic (but not too basic) Expressions

Aye – Yes

Now – No

Yah and Nay -   Yes and No (when contradicting)

Sithee - Behold

'Ey Up - Hello/Well I never/ Please move over

Tha Wa'? - 'Pardon?

Dust? – Do You?

Ast? – Have You?

Art? – Are You?

Uz'll – We Will

Worrell? - What will?

Them'll -They will

Owdonabit – Just one Moment Please

Worrizit? – Can I help you?

Speighk Proper! – You are not using the correct Lancashire vernacular!

~~~

Lanky Table Etiquette — some Do's and Don'ts.

They do things differently in Lancashire. To a Lancastrian, lunchtime is dinnertime and dinnertime is teatime. Got that? It is very important to remember that if invited to someone's home for dinner, you go at lunchtime, whereas if it's a teatime invitation, you go at dinner time. Otherwise, if you're not careful, you could end up with no dinner at 'teatime', no lunch at 'dinner time'- and tea with just about everything.

MANNERS!

When slurping soup, do try to keep the noise down to reasonable proportions, i.e. slightly less than that of a 747 taking off.

Never drink brown sauce straight from the bottle - you never know who may have been drinking out of it before you.

Do not flick mushy peas at the waiter to attract his attention - they may stick in his ears be won't be able to hear your order.

Do you leave a tip? Of course — no one likes eating in a tip.

It is not the done thing in Lancashire to cool one's red-hot tea by blowing on it in the cup. The correct procedure is to pour it into the saucer and fan it gently with a cloth-cap.

Always make sure of what you are eating - if the brown bread turns out to be hard, it could be that you've just buttered and eaten three table-mats.

When eating black puddings, always use fingers preferably your own. Never wipe your greasy fingers on the tablecloth — stroke the dog under the table instead.

You can safely drink the water. Most Lancastrians enjoy drinking water in huge quantifies - usually in conjunction with hops and malted barley.

Never use a napkin - tuck the tablecloth into your collar instead. That 'way, if you inadvertently drop a slippy length of tripe, it will slither its own way down back on to the plate.

~~~

EATING OUT IN LANCASHIRE

Yisluv?

I am ready to take your order, sir

Mi belly thinks me throoat's cut

By Jove, I am ready to eat something

Ah cud eight a scabby pig beawt bread

Ah cud eight a flock bed

Ah cud eight a keaw (cow) between two bread vans

I am extremely hungry

Shape thisel

Arryup serry

Waiter - please act with more celerity

Ah'm o'erfaced

The abundance of food has taken away my appetitite

This is gradely snap/jackbit/meight

This is good food

Fotch three cheers

There are three of us. We require three chairs

Yon steak's as big as a fly's left nadger

They give rather small portions in this establishment

That's rather moorish

I could eat some more of that

Ah wur fair clemmt

I was rather peckish

Stop thi' gollopin – there's two prizes

Take your time with that food

Stop slavverin

Please keep your mouth from drooling

Wheerst petty?

Could you direct me to the convenience please?

Babbies' yeds

(ie Babies' heads – ie Steak puddings, because of their shape).

Blanket Lifters

Baked beans/ Black Peas or legumes in general

Prayter Cakes

Potato Cakes

Slavvery Duck

Savoury Duck – a herby/offally Lancashire "delicacy"

Feesh

Fish

Fotchuzafeeshfrumtchippywilta?

Would you please bring me a fish from the chipshop?

Shives o' bread

Slices of bread

Dooersteps

Thick slices of bread

Beighultam

Boiled Ham

Sawt

Salt

Maggy-ann

Margarine

Ap-puhs

Apples

Barm Joe

Barm Cake

Crusses

Crusts – (them as allegedly make your hair curl if you eat plenty of them)

Pidjin Peighs

Black peas – a tasty Lancashire dish seen at fairs or wakes's and at bonfires

Tommy-taters

Tomatoes

Pobs

Pieces of bread and with sugar in hot milk. Food for invalids..

Sterrie/Sturrer

Sterilised milk

Keaw Milk

Pasteurised as opposed to sterilized

Tin-lally Butty

Condensed Milk sandwich. Not recommended by dentists

Ah cud murder a pon o' lobby

I could just eat a pan of lobscouse (thought to be a Liverpool delicacy but a variant is very popular in Lancashire)

Singing Lily

Flat cake crammed with currants

Corporation Pop

Water

Gracie Chips

Greasy chips

Waiter!

Bring me a glass of water quick!

This tay's like gnat pee

This tay's too wake (weak) to come eawt o't pot

This tea isn't very strong

Side table

You may clear the table, waiter

Ah'm stawed

I am full up

Owtelse?

Do you require anything else?

Yer con shuv that wheer't monkeys shove their nuts

That bill is rather excessive

~~~

Useful Equipment to Take on Your Expedition to Deepest Lancashire

STOUT PAIR OF CLOGS – as used by Lancashire philosophers for putting across the point of an argument.

SAW – for sawing the knocker-upper's pole in half when you fancy a lie-in in the morning.

(A knocker upper isn't what outsiders might think he is. He is, or rather was, a man who was employed to go round first thing in the morning with a long pole banging on windows in the days when people were too poor to afford alarm clocks. Those days could yet come back)

SHOVEL - handy for shoveling coal out of boarding house bath before filling with water

NEEDLE AND COTTON - useful for sewing your ears back on with after arguing with a Rugby League prop-forward in a pub.

SMALL TERRIER - useful for shoving down your trousers in case a ferret runs up your leg.

MACKINTOSH, WELLINGTONS, UMBRELLA, LIFEBELT - in case the weather takes a turn for the better.

CHIP PAN - which Lancastrians use on their heads as crash-helmets.

PHOTO OF YORKSHIREMAN - for making black puddings easier to eat: it scares them out of their skins.

ST BERNARD DOG WITH BARREL OF BEST BITTER ROUND NECK - in case you get stranded all night on a slag heap.

WHIPPET-BITE SERUM - for people who go round biting whippets.

~~~

Deawn Th'Aleheawse*

*At the Public House

The taproom of a pub is one of the greatest repositories of Lancashire dialect. It is a place where the Lancastrian feels most at his ease and the language flows freely along with the ale. To hear Lanky spoken proper and see the natives in their natural habitat, visit a taproom or some cosy little Victorian pub.

Freeman's ale's best

That beer is best which is bought for one

Ah'm brastin fer a sup

I am extremely thirsty

A pint o' flatrib

A pint of dark mild

A gill o' bit-ther

A half-pint of bitter

Geeuza pint o' girder

I would like a pint of Guinness, landlord.

(This drink is reputed to have tumescent properties)

Bones

Dominoes

Arrers

Darts

Bowels

Crown green bowls (also known as woods)

This ale's aw rest fur purrin' on chips

Landlord, your beer tastes like vinegar

Don't sup that, It'll blow thi bally-button off

Put that keg beer down

A breawn split

Brown ale mixed with bitter or mild

This ale tastes lahk maiden's-waiter

It is extremely weak

It's lahk gnatpee

Like I said - it's extremely weak

Wiv stopped some ale fra gooin' seawr

Wiv ginnit some stick

We have consumed a goodly quantity of beer

'Ee's takkin a sweetener wom

He is taking home a bottle of beer in order to ingratiate himself with his wife, because he has been out too long

'Ee's a reet ale-can

He is a potential alcoholic

Brewer's goitre

Pot-belly through consuming too much beer

Backer

Tobacco

Smooks

Cigarettes

Ee smooks lahk a fackthry chimbley

He smokes like a factory chimney

They'n signed him 'igh

He's been banned sine die from a club

Ee's playin' him

He has absconded from work

Ah'm short o' dosh

I have no money

Ast geet a latchlifter?

Can you lend me enough money to enable me to buy the first pint?

Ah've ad a boatload

I'm full of beer

This is fer 'oo kissis Betty

This is to decide who is the overall winner (at darts, dominoes, etc)

Ahm on a promise

My wife has designated tonight to grant me her sexual favours

It's lahk payin' to a chance-child

The price of this beer is extortionate

'Is tap's stopped

The landlord is refusing to serve him (Or His wife is denying him his conjugal rights)

Ee no clack in 'im. His legs is 'oller

He is a prodigious drinker

It's a smookjack/smooker

That was marvellous

(of a good dart/goal/bowl, etc)

Yer con bet Connie's odds

Nothing is more certain

Ah'll gam onnit

I will bet money on it

Gerremminagen!

Landlord, please replenish our glasses!

Eez spewed iz ring up

He has been sick all over the carpet

(otherwise known as 'shouting for Hughie' after the 'EEOOIE 'sound it makes)

Speak up Brown - you're through!

Said after someone has 'broken wind,' 'dropped one,' 'cut their finger,' 'let Polly out of prison', 'trumped,' etc.

She'll do it fer peanuts then come back fer't shells

A reference to a woman of loose morals

It came away like a flock o' sparrows

A reference to loose bowels caused by a surfeit of drinking

E's peed aw 'is munny agenst waw

Ee's drunk us a fiddler's foo

He has spent all his money on beer

Ee 's drunk as a mop

Ee's getten a sweigh on

Ee's drunk as a monkey

He is extremely drunk

Sod this fer a game o' sowjers

I don't intend carrying on along these lines

Chukkin eawt tahm

Closing time

Avyernowomsgutto?!

Time gentlemen, please!

Ah'll see thi't morn morn

I'll see you tomorrow morning

Ah've bin ta'n short. Ah'll affert empty mi clog.

I will have to go to the toilet -

That's peed on't chips

That's very unfortunate,

Strap it

I will pay for it at a later date

Ah'm gooin fert shake honds wi't best mon at mi weddin'

Ah'm gooin' shake dew off me lily

Ah'm brastin for a slash

I simply must visit the gents

Pie—eyed... Slat at...Kalied...Piddelt...Slewed tert gills...Tanked up...Sozzlt...Skennin moppin' drunk

Really Drunk!

~~~

How to Recognise a Lanky Chauvinist Pig (L.C.P.)

Though Lancastrians are by nature warm and friendly - unlike the climate - as in any society, you may meet the occasional bigot who is ill-disposed to outsiders: usually Southern shandy-supping 'jessies' and Yorkshire 'puddings.

I have christened such a being the Lanky Chauvinist Pig. This is how to recognise him:

He always carries two short planks under his arm to illustrate what he thinks a Yorkshireman is as thick as.

He uses toilet-paper with pictures of William Hague, Michael Parkinson and Geoff Boycott on.

He never asks your opinion about Lancashire - he *tells* you.

His wife always walks three paces behind him – (with a big whip in her hand.)

He has a soft spot for Southerners — the quicksands at Morecambe Bay.

He breaks wind loudly, then blames it on the dog.

He thinks P.C. is the local bobby.

He says the best road in Yorkshire is the one leading to Lancashire.

He thinks the ideal method of birth control is keeping a ferret in bed.

He reckons the chip-pan is the greatest invention since the wheel

That's him drinking your ale.

~~~

Th'Insults (use sparingly and with discretion.. Think of your teeth)

Ee's as useless as a one-legged mon at an arse-kicking contest.

He's not much good at anything.

Tha'rt as thick as a Wiggin butty

Tha'rt as dim as a TocH lamp

Tha'rt thick as pigmuck

Tha'rt numm as a pit-prop

You seem to have a very low IQ.

Th'art nowt an' nowt'll become o' thi an' aw thi 'air'll drop eawt

You are very wicked and you will come to nothing and all your hair will drop out

(a frightening warning of a semi-prophetic nature to a bad person)

Thezza mahnd like a muck-midden

You are of a coarse nature

Thezza yedfull o' jolly robins

You are nothing but a daydreamer

Yurra big soft tatah – yer Mary Ann.

You are somewhat effeminate

Ah'm tawkln tert th'organ-grahnder - norriz munkey

Ah'm tawkln tert th'enjin-drahver - norriz rubbin-rag

You are of no consequence - I am speaking to people who know more about these things than you do

He con get wheer weyter cawnt

He can get where water cant (i.e. everywhere; a half-grudging, half-jealous remark about a person who does well through his efforts at dealing with people)

Thurr nowt burn load o' rang-tang

They are a rubbishy bunch of fellows

Art tryin't pee up mi back?

Are you trying to get one over on me?

When theaw wur born, thi shudda kept th'afterbirth an thrown't babby away

The midwife who brought you into the world did it a disservice

Thaz too much o' that what cat licks its arse wi

You talk too much

Ee'd skin a flea for awpni. (halfpenny)

'Ee wuddn't, gi thi't steam offizpee

If eeda gobful o' gumbeighls, e wuddn't part wi' one

That man is mean

'Ee wouldn't pee on you If you wur burnin'

He is not a very helpful fellow

Pig off, yer greyt eggwap

You are a fool - please go away

Stop thi' tollerin

Desist from showing off

Huh - theer guz Little Miss Keck

That girl is very full of herself

Ah bet thy teeth're glad when tha'rt asleep

You don't hail talk a great deal

Who's getten thee ready? Thi mam?

Insulting remark to a well-dressed person

'Ee thinks it's fer stirring 'is tay with.

He thinks it's for stirring his tea with: (a slighting reference to a sexually inexperienced male)

Ee's proper monkified

He is very mischievous

Tell't truth and shoam't devil (Tell the truth and shame the devil)

You tell lies

Tha'rt proper mard thy art

You are spoiled and childish

Gutter hell an' pump at thunder

Shove off

Bumpin' weight

A curious adjectival term usually tagged on to an obscene noun beginning with the letter C.

Tha'rt an idle scrawp

You are a lazy so-and-so

The following names all mean roughly the same thing, i.e. a fool, and should only be used when speaking to a person of a much smaller stature (preferably one -legged midget), or when the person delivering the insult can boast some degree of efficiency in the martial arts:

Tha'rt nowt burra...

You are nothing but a.

Slavverin' foo...Snowbaw...Crate-egg...Warpyed...Noan reet bugga...Bladder-yed...Stonejug...Slobbergob...Eighl-can...Ponyed...Snorin' Crow...Rubbin' Rag...Barmpot

There, you've said it — now run like blazes!

~~~

Feightin' Tawk
*Fighting Talk

If you're feeling particularly belligerent, try a few of these:

On yer bike serry!

Despatch yourself hence!

Tha'll cop it neaw

You are for it my friend

Th'art nowt a peawnd (You are nothing-a-pound)

I am not afraid of you

Ah'll spit in thi eye an' bugblind thi

I am about to become aggressive

There's moor bant in a wet lettuce

You are a weakling

Ah'll banjo thee

You have no chance against my superior fighting powers

Dust want a knuckle butty?

Would you like to taste my fist?

Tha's a face lahk a joss-arsed baboon

You are no oil-painting

Ah'll cleawt thi' lug'ole

I am aiming to land a blow on your ear

Ah'll mollycrush thee

I will totally annihilate you

Ah'll parr thi yed in

I intend to kick your cranium in

Ah'll paste thi ear'ole

I'll flatten your ear for you

Th'arz a face as long as a gasmon's mac

You are as ugly as a gas meter reader's attire (when they had distinctive long coats)

If 'ee 'ad any moor meawth, 'eed 'ave no face left ter wesh

If his mouth was any bigger, he would have no face left to wash   -

'Ees lahk a dog wi' a tin dick

'Ees lahk a dog wi' two dicks

He is extremely pleased

Gerrim gelded!

Drastic measures are needed to curb him

If tha doesn't gerrup quick, I'll cum'n pee in thi earhole!

Shouted upstairs as an encouragement for someone to get out of bed

Ahlommerthi

I will hammer you

Ah'll beeyit thi

I will beat you

Ah'll skutch thi legs

I will scrape your legs

Tha cuddn't lick a toffee apple

You've no chance in a fight

Dust wanna Wigan Kiss?

Would you like me to butt you in the face?

Ah'll punch thi supper up

This next blow is aimed at your abdomen

Ah'll parr thi shins till tha skrikes

I will kick your shins till you cry out loud.

Dustgeeup?

Have you had enough?

~~~

Some Affectionate Terms

Owd Beigh…Owd Beighzer…Buggerlugs…Brid…Cocker…Fettler…Owd Lad…Owd Luv…Owd Jockey…Skimbo…Sticker…Owd Stockin'…Owd Stockin Top…Owd Sparrer…Owd Shugger Butty…Owd Scholar…Owd Prater…Owd Prater Pie…

To be used only when you have gained the utmost respect, familiarity and affection of a Lancastrian, such as when you've bought him a pint in a pub.

In Lancashire, you can address someone as "cock" without getting battered. "Love" is also used frequently even if you've just met the woman. Shopgirls use it a lot to customers. Sometimes men call each other love and no-one bats an eyelid. Except strangers.

Lancastrians know they are truly home when they are being called "cock" and "love".

"Love" has another useful purpose. When someone addresses you in the street by your first name and asks "How arta?" and you can't for the life of you think who they are, the response "Am awreet luv, thanks for askin'" will get you out of the predicament.

The letter "R" is, strangely, a term of affection too. As in R Kid, R Albert or R Kylie.

The word 'thee' can be used as a term to express real affection in such phrases as **'Ee ah luv thee,'** or **'Ah've tekken ter thee'** but it can also be most insulting when used offensively, as when speaking to someone older than you are or in aggressive circumstances, such as **'Oi thee Ah'll punch thi nose tert back o' thi face!'**

When used in unfortunate circumstances and the recipient feels offended, he will usually respond with:

'Don't thee thee me thee. Thee thee thisel and see how thee likes it!'

~~~

Beighin' Clooers *

*Buying clothes.

Anyerany…?

Have you got any…?

Gollies

Galoshes

Nebbers

Peaked flat caps

Dolly 'ats

Bowler hats

Cozzies

Bathing costumes

Cardies

Cardigans

Shoon

Shoes

Canal Barges

Large shoes

Snotrags

Handkerchiefs

Brats

Aprons

Kecks

Knickers or Trousers

Britches

Trousers

Mufflers

White Scarves

Sherts

Shirts

Ganzies

Jumpers

Jarmers

Pyjamas

Galluses

Braces.

Dirt is another name for workclothes – as in:

"Tha cawn't come in here in thi dert!"

~~~

Deawn at Doc's*

*Visiting the Doctor

Some Lanky expressions that you may hear wafting through the doctor's surgery door…

Are theaw't quack?

Excuse me, are you the doctor?

Ah feel wake

I feel weak

Ah keep gooin' mazey

I am continually having dizzy spells

Ah'm aw cowd crills

I am shivering

Ah varnear collopst

I have nearly collapsed

Ah'm reet jiggered

I am tired out through effort

Ah'm eawt o' flunther

I feel out of condition

(this word is also used to denote some piece of apparatus is not functioning properly)

Ah'm cowfin lahk a good-un

I can't seem to stop coughing

Ah'm powfagged

I'm weary/browbeaten

Ah'm two double wi't bellywarch

I am doubled up with stomach pains

Ah've getten yedwarch

My head aches

'Ees ta'n bad roads

The patient is getting worse

Ahm bun up

I am constipated. (**eggbun** is the state of being constipated through eating too many eggs)

Ah'm still a bit tickle

I am still not quite right

Ah've a spile in mi ond

I have a splinter in my hand

Ah cud do wi summat purra road through me

Please prescribe me a laxative (also known as oppenin'-medicine)

Ah've summat in mi een

I have something in my eye

Ah'm stuffed-up to buggery wi a cowd   .

I'm full of a cold

Ah feel lahk a furnist (furnace)

I am running a temperature

Mi guts're off

I have tummy trouble

Mi gob tastes lahk th'inslde uv a Turkish wrestler's jockstrap

I have halitosis

Cough it up — it met be a pianner! (might be a piano)

Get it off your chest (phlegm)

Ah think ah'm mendin

I am getting much better

Chickenpots

Chickenpox

It's summat an' nowt

You'll survive

Ah'm swettin' lahk a pig

I have a perspiration problem

Purruz on't club wilta doc?

I wish to receive benefits

~~~

Jobs

Skoomester

Schoolmaster

Sowjer

Soldier

Wakesmon

Fairground worker

Torchy

Cinema usher

Lekkymon

Electricity meter reader

Buzz Dreighver

Bus driver

Chukker-eawter

Bouncer

Parkie

Park keeper

Clubmon

Insurance collector

Lurry Dreighver

Lorry driver

Binmon,

Refuse collector

Owd septic knuckles

The rent man/ Debt Collector

Rozzer\ Bluebottle

Policeman

Papperlad

Newsboy

Mitherin' Bugger

Cold caller at your door.

~~~

Features – looks aren't everything.

We have a way of describing folk in Lancashire and it's not always very complimentary…

'Ees as thin as a Nooner wi' one meetin' in it

He's very thin

(refers to midday edition of racing-paper with only one race meeting and therefore only a couple of pages)

'Er's a face lahk a busted clog/a melted welly/ a ruptured custard

She isn't very pretty

'Ee's as fow as a summons

He is ugly and unwanted

(fow or feaw can mean ugly - of a person or place - and also lucky. . . as in 'yer fow divil,' meaning 'you lucky devil')

It favvers a sod reawnd a rat-hole

Why cultivate on thi' face what grows wild reawnd thi' arse?

Pejorative term relating to a person's moustache

'Ey Fatrops!

An attempt to attract a portly gentleman's attention

'Er looks lahk a bag o' muck teed in't middle wi a piece o' string

Said of an unshapely woman in a dress

Snot carpet

The distance between one's nostrils and one's top lip

Eez up and down lahk a prostitute's pants

Eez up and down lahk a fartinabottle

He is very restless

Eez lahk a fart in a cullinder

He doesn't know which way to turn

Eez geet eyes lahk rissoles in the snow

A euphemism for someone whose eyes have taken on a sunken appearance

Ast getten sum muck on thi' top lip?

Asked of person with look of distaste on face

Tha'art a reet toe-rag

You are a most unworthy person

Yon mon con whisper o'er three fields – Huddersfield, Sheffield and Macclesfield.

That fellow has an exceptionally loud voice

'Ee walks lahk a ruptured duck

He does not walk normally

Oi Rag-eye!

I say you with the eye defect!

'Ee's a face uz'd stond cloggin'

He is most hard-faced

'Ee cud walk under th'essole wi a top hat on (esshole is the part of the fire where ashes drop)

He is very small

Ah cud eight them beawt bread (eat them without bread)

That young lady has a buxom appearance

'Ee favvers a strake o' pee on a whiteweshed waw

Isn't he thin?

'Er's getten sparrerlegs

She has extremely thin legs

'Eigh, thee wi't pastie-feet

Excuse me, the gentleman with the large feet! (like very large Gregg's pasties)

It's surprisin' what yer see when yer eawt beawt gun (out without your gun)

That's a very unusual-looking person

Art breighkin' um in fer an 'orse?

Reference to large teeth

Ten ter two feet

Feet splayed out in V-shape

'Ee cudn't stop a pig in a ginnel

He is bowlegged

Shut thi gob an' gi' thi' arse a chance

I fear you are monopolising the conversation

'Ee cud carry fahve peawnd o' King Edwards iniz cap

He has an unusually large head

'Ees as randy as a booardin'-eawse tomcat

He is of an amorous nature

'As sumbdi cut thi' 'air wi a knahf un fork?

Your barber's tonsorial capabilities leave much to be desired.

'Ee int hawf ballyin' eawt

His abdomen is getting bigger

'Er's as fawce as a ferret

She is cunning

Tha'rt as black as up chimney/ black as an ousel (blackbird)

Why don't you have a wash?

'Ere's mi yed, mi arse is cummin

Applied to a person who walks in a bustling manner with head to the fore

~~~

All Together Now!

Lancashire words have a tendency to run all together. This may confuse the unaccustomed ear but it does save time that is unless you have to explain to the unaccustomed ear what it was you were saying in the first place.

Willy Eckerslike

He will not

Avennyonyerennyonyer?

Have any of you any on you? (matches, cigarettes, money, etc.)

Weyntajust?Theeseeiffadon't

Oh won't I? You will see!

Wivgettentgutsleep

We have to go to sleep

Artshoorothat?

Are you positive?

Aberragerralorravum

I bet I get a lot of them

Azzyettenworrizgetten?

Has he eaten what he's got?

Weeaffertguffertbuzz

We must leave now - our bus is due

Astnottellthitwahce

I won't repeat myself.

Purrasockinnitwilta?

Shut up

Amgooinwomburrallbibackinabit

I am going home but will soon return

Yacht?

Is it too warm in here for you?

Astbinmenbinmam?

Have the refuse collectors called yet, mother?

Lukkatyeddonthat!

Look at the size of his head!

~~~~

Swurr Wurds*

*Expletives

Ecky pecky thump! (very mild)

Skennin' eck! (tame)

By the stars! (innocuous)

By the crin! (permissible in polite company)

Ah'll go ter the foot of eawr sturrs! (traditional)

Flamin' Nora! (Who was she?)

Ah'll go ter mi tay! (inoffensive)

Flamin' Hanover!! (slightly stronger)

Owd mon!! (a reference to the devil?)

By the roastin mon!! (the devil again?)

Blood and sand!! (moderate)

Blood and stomach pills!! (rather forced)

Jerr-usalem! (slightly profane — a vicar-shocker)

Buggamee ! !! (very strong)

Hells Bells of Buggery!!!!! (use only under extreme provocation — and don't let your mother hear you.)

(Yes I know. There's worse said on telly these days).

~~~

Sayin's

The traveller will frequently be bemused by various 'sayings' which the native Lancastrian is fond of trotting out, and which usually encapsulate some grain of truth.

In the event of being unable to understand the speaker, the traveller is advised to nod knowingly and sympathetically and act as though he has been the recipient of some great truth. You *may* have been for all you know.

Tha con treighed on't cat till it turns on thi

You can tread on a cat until it turns on you- You can only push a person so far

Wheer thurs least room, thurs mooerst thrutchin'

People who criticise other people should have regard to their own faults first

A big knocker sets a dooer off

A big nose gives a face character- (usually said by people with big noses)

It's gone wheer it's ned (needed)

Said grudgingly of someone who has had a windfall

God's good ter gobbins

The Good Lord protects the simple-minded

Tha'rt clever but tha'll dee

You may be more intelligent than I am, but you will still die anyway

'Ee's getten moor in is yed than nits

He has more in his head than nits- He is very clever

It weynt eight grass

It won't eat grass

A rather low reference to the female pudendum in a period of separation from boyfriend or husband; indicates the speaker thinks he has a chance of 'scoring'

He'd gi thi his arse an' shit through his ribs

He is a most generous person

~~~

The Weather

We have a lot of weather in Lancashire. Here are some sayings connected with it.

It favvers cowd eawt

It seems to be cold outside

It's fleein

It is most inclement

It's teeminorain

Heighvin' deawn

Peltin deawn

Chukkin it deawn

Cummin deawn i' bukkitfuls

Peeindeawn

Doin' sum

Like stair-rods.

It is raining very hard

It's slutchy

It is muddy

Amfrozzendeeuth

Brr — I'm very cold

It's cowd enough fer two pair o' socks

It's really cold

Ahm sogginweet throo

My clothes are drenched

Owd Sol's eawt!

Hurray - the sun is shining!

It's crackintflags

Now that's what I call hot!

Not forgetting "It's that fine rain what wets yer"

So it does!

~~~

Useful Words and Phrases…. Plus odds'n'sods

(Chuck these in the conversation and they'll think you're a native)

Varnear

Nearly

Ah cawnt win a kest

I can't win anything

Keck o'er

Topple over

Its aw up-brew

It's all uphill

Sex

Sacks

Bingo's loosin'

The bingo hall is emptying

Mee-maw

To make faces at or gesture behind someone's back

Mank abeawt

Act the fool

Chelp

Impertinence

Lozz

Lay about indolently

Had up

Summonsed by the court

Grotch/Golly/Goz/Gob

Expectorate

Gawm

To recognise, acknowledge someone

Chunner

Mutter, natter at someone

Turr-arse abeawt

Rush about

A reet knicker-gripper

A frightening situation, like an X-rated film or a visit from your mad auntie.

Muck er nettles

All or nothing

Up at crack o' sparrowfart

To rise early

Sprag

To bolster up

Duck muck

Mucus in eye from sleeping

It's a bus rahd off

It is a fair distance

Nobbut a cockstride

Near

Yonmon

Him

Wazzums

Worms

Rootin and Tootin

Being inquisitive

Rawin' an Mawin'

Struggling with something

O'erlied   .   . .

Overslept

A midgy's. widgy off

A bug's dick off

Very close

Spiggy/ Spuggy

Spearmint \ Chewing Gum

Wap one on

Put one on (as in Wap a sausage on't barbecue)

Ahmet

Not a foreign name it means 'I might'

Nannyin'

Illicit love

Pog

Steal (as in poggin' ap-puhs – stealing apples)

Owt abeawt owt abeawt!

Expression of disbelief

Wur poo'd eawt (Pulled out)

We are very busy

Farnitcher

Furniture

Ah've gorra lassoo

I've got a girl who

Ah seedit!

I saw it!

Tha never sez/ Ah cawnt Speyk!

I don't believe it!

Backerts an forrerts

Backwards and forwards

Is thi' clugs clent?

Are your clogs cleaned?

Grawl

To molest a young lady on a date

Tissue papper ears

Said of someone who hears what they're not supposed to hear

Ahlsitmieer

I will sit down here

Ah keep gooin' wi't yed deawn (with the head down)

I struggle through life. This is heard a lot

Art cooertin?

Are you seeing a member of the opposite sex?

Tha'rt slow us a Godshorse

You are extremely tardy

They'n flit

The persons you seek have moved house

Pots fer rags

Silly

Farriners

Newcomers to a district

Ah'm fast!

I am stuck!

Frikky!

You are a scaredy-cat

Setdi

Saturday

Moggy

Mouse or tiny insect in some parts of Lancashire. Cat in others. Strange that.

Nowtyback

Naughty child

It stunk mon's height

It smelled a great deal- ie to the height of a man

Th'owd mon

Strangely said endearingly of a youngster

Ah wur cawed gooin' wom

I was supposed to be going home

Th'owd stockin'-mender

The wife

Pow

Haircut

Pow-slap

An old Lancashire custom whereby a person who has just had a haircut is given a slap on the back of the neck

Rucks/Ruckins

Slag heaps

Razzer

Reservoir

Thrutch

A beautiful all-purpose word meaning to strain or push. Can also mean to strain on the lavatory due to the effects of being constipated. "Ah were thrutchin' but nowt happened".

Sloppy daw-daw

Child's name for mud

Bobby's winder (window)

A hole in a stocking

Dustyarmi?

Can you hear me?

Crabby/Crawpy/Jammy/Spawny

Lucky

Stop gerrinagate o' mi!

Please stop annoying me!

Purler/Blahnder/Dormer/Belter!

Good one!

Eawf-soaked

Slow-witted

Ahm not coddin', it wur rotten good

I deceive you not it was brilliant

Peg eawt/ Dee

Die

Peg up

Lift someone up by their leg to enter a window or climb a fence

It's a beltin' little tenter

It is a very good guard dog

~~~

Eee It's a Lowf Innit!

'Witticisms' yer might hear out and about...

Take care when riding a bicycle through the streets of Lancashire. The following shouts can be heard frequently coming from children:

Gerroff an' milk it!

Get off and milk it!

Eigh - dust know thi back wheel's follerin' thi' frunt un?

Do you realise your back wheel is following your front one?

Whooz deed?

Who has died? Said to a person with trouser-leg bottoms above their ankles, i.e. half mast

Q: What con ah haft eight mam? What can I eat, mother?

A: Three run jumps up buttery dooer an when tha gets theer, slurr deawn

Three running jumps up the pantry door - and when you get there, slide down

Q: What's that tha'rt making? What are you making?

A: Layholes fer meddlers an' crutches for lame ducks

Nonsense phrase intended to rebuff stupid question

Tha'll bi lahk Morty's Donkey

This is said to be a person who refuses to eat his food, it refers to an apocryphal tale about a certain man named Mort who had just got his donkey used to living without food when surprisingly it died

Th'art up early - ast peedibed?

Said to an early riser, it insinuates that the person has risen for reasons other than the desire to be up early

Crows'll mess on yer

Said of someone who has no new clothes for Easter - it arises out of the superstition that the crows single out such unfortunate people and 'spot' them

Ey thee-cum here!

And when the dupe all unsuspectingly returns, the joker quips merrily:

Eeaw far wutta bin if theaw hadn't come back?

How far would you have been if you hadn't come back? To which the dupe replies, if he is of razor- sharp mentality:

Twice length uv a foo' (fool). Lie deawn while ah measure thi'

The biter bit!

Q: Who is it? Who's theer? A:Icky –t'fire bobby

A mythical Lancashire personality. It's said in a "mind your own business" sort of way.

Q:Is it rainin?

To someone who is drenched

A: No, ah've Just pooered a bukkit o' waiter o'er mi yed.

No - I've just poured a bucket of water over my head (sarcastic retort)

Q: Warrat gawpin' at?

What are you looking at?

A: Ah dunno - label's dropped off

Q: Ast getten thi eenfull?

Have you got your eye full?

A: Aye

A: Well turn reawnd and get t'other full

Q: Dust wanna picture?

A: (Either) **No ta - ah don't collect 'orrer pictures. (Or) Aye - It'll do fer frikkenin' (frightening) cats off petty waw (lavatory wall)**

Gerreawt o't leet — tha weren't made I' St Helens

Get out of the light - you were not made in St Helens

Said to someone obstructing a person's view, it refers to the glass that St Helens is famous for manufacturing

Bi sharp theer an back, an if tha faws, don't stop gerrup

Be quick there and back, and if you fall, don't stop to getup.

Think about it...

Skoobell's gone

The schoolbell has sounded

A: Whooz tan it?! Who's taken it?

This witty response loses something in the translation.

Tha'rt gooin't meet thiself cummin back

Slow down

Put thi' torch eawt .— it's meltin' mi ice lolly!

Facetious cry to usherette in cinema

UNSUSPECTING TRAVELLER: I I say there, you chappy - have you got a match?

WITTY LANKY MON: Aye - thy face an my arse.

~~~

On't Road – Lanky Road Signs

DRIVE SLOWLY
– COBBLED MOTORWAY

WATCH OUT
– MOTHER-IN-LAW
AHEAD . . .

YORKSHIRE CRICKET FANS
AFTER LOSING ROSES
MATCH

BEWARE – RACING PIGEONS
OVERHEAD!

PEDESTRIAN
CLOGDANCING . . .

LANCASHIRE CRICKET FANS
AFTER WINNING ROSES
MATCH

LANCASHIRE WELCOMES
SOUTHERN DRIVERS

ROAD SIGNS

You will encounter a number of strange
road signs whilst travelling around
Lancashire. Here are some to keep your
eyes open for . . .

TOILETS

YOU ARE ILLEGALLY
PARKED ON A RUGBY
LEAGUE PITCH

LAST BLACK PUDDING STOP
BEFORE M.1.

A POEM

There's no doubt that the Lancashire landscape has changed a great
deal since Lanky Spoken Here was first published in the 70's.
Gone are most of the mills and mines which provided the lifeblood
of employment for thousands of Lancastrians.
When the factory chimney belonging to Howe Bridge Mills at the
corner of Mealhouse Lane and Bag Lane in my old home town of
Atherton was knocked down, I went to watch.
There were scores of people there including some, I imagine, who
had worked at the mill and who came away more than a little heavy-
hearted and sad that this familiar landmark had been taken away. It
reminded us that the cotton industry which, along with the pits, had
been the life-blood of the town was in decline and it was one less
link with the past.
It reminded me of a public execution. So I attributed a personality to
the old chimney and went home and wrote this poem in memory of
it.

FOR A DOOMED FACTORY CHIMNEY.

Creawds o' folk have come fert watch thi dee,
Owd familiar friend.
Th'art useless and unwanted dosta see.
Thi life mun end.

 Preawd tha stonds like one o't th'upper crust.
Soon tha'll be gone.
And of thi memory, there'll be nowt but dust.
Like mortal mon.

For years tha played a leading part on't stage
And played it well.
And saw th'awf-timers through to ripe owd age
Just like thisel.

Whene'er tha breathed, tha breathed life into't place
But that's in't past.

When Progress says "I dunnot like thy face"
Tha's breathed thi last.

Here comes thi executioner deawnt street.
Thi life is dun wi.
I'm sure tha'd try't escape if tha'd but geet
Some legs fert run wi.

Creawds hushed and silent neaw and then comes one
Almighty crack.
Tha topples o'er and then tha's gone
Wi brokken back.

And th'eyes that watched thi faw neaw fill wi tears.
Folk realise.
Theaw were a symbol o' their workin' years.
Neaw dead tha lies.

An epitaph fer thee I've written deawn
I'll say it clear.
Here lies t'body of a forgotten cotton teawn
RIP Lancashire.

~~~

ANOTHER POEM

OWD THRUMBLE'S OWD THROMBOOAN

(Winner of the Lancashire Dialect Society Poetry Competition)

Brass bands are a great feature of Lancashire life. In their own way, they contribute so much to the culture and the atmosphere of a town. On a walking day, when the churches, chapels and Sunday schools parade, the first you know that the "scholars" are approaching is when you hear the strains of the band in the distance. "DAH-DAH-DA-DA (DA-DA!); DAH-DAH-DA-DA (DA-DA!)" You know the tune I mean?

The crowd ready themselves for the procession. Then you see the banners above the heads of the spectators floating in the air like the sails of a galleon... Mind you, you can't help laughing when it's a windy day and the banner carriers struggle to keep their feet. But it's the band seems to set everything up just right. This poem was loosely based on a gentleman called Bert who played trombone in a brass band and lived at the end of our terraced row. Poetic licence has been taken with the facts.

There's an owd mon lives at th'eend o't street
We know as just "Owd Thrumble"
He's a mon who dun't ameawnt ter much
In fact he's nobbut 'umble.

Yer wouldn't turn yer yed fert gawp
If yer walked past him in't lone.
But the thing as folks all know him fer
Is Owd Thrumble's owd thrombooan.

Cos him and his owd insthrument
Are two peighs in a swod.
He'd rayther part wi't missis
Than part wi that, by God.

And when there's nowt on't telly
Or't weather's ooercast,
He teks his owd thrombooan eawt
And he dun't hawf lerrit brast!

His lungs is lahk two bellowses
And his lips is made o' flint.
He blows that 'ard deawnt meawthpiece
As it meks his eyebaws squint.

His faces terns blue, and his tung does too
As't blood to his yed goes rushin'
And his cheeks swell eawt lahk casebaws
Mon! He'd frikken Peter Cushin'!

Black Dyke and Brigeawse, Bessies too,
He's played wi't best of aw.
But they secks him, cos his high-notes
Meks aw't plaster faw off't waw.

Ter't Silver and Brass enthusiasts
He's known througheawt the land
And they caw 'im "Owd Titanic"-
Cos he dreawns aw't rest o't band.

When he comes fra werk, he has his tay,
Then eawt cums th'owd thrombooan,
An fer two-thri eawrs, he worries it
Lahk a bulldog wi a booan.

At hawf past eight, he pikes off pub
And staggers wom at ten
Then he gets his owd thrombooan eawt-
And lets it brast agen!

One neet, he staggered wom from't pub
Wi a booatload under't skin
E sucked instead o' blowin't thrombooan-
An 'oovered t'babby in!

His wahf leet eawt a piercin' skrike
And't neighbours yerd her sheawt
"Wist hafta send a ferret deawn
Fert get the bugger eawt!"

When Thrumble's tryin't practice scales,
It's lahk a donkey brayin'
An next dooer's dog jumps straight deawn't bog
And th'ens have aw stopped layin'.

Tha couldn't caw 'is music "canned",
It's rayther moor like "tinned"
It seawnds just like a helephant
What's troubled bad wi't wind.

Ah feels sorry fer 'is family-
Fer them there's no relief.
Poor budgy's awlus yedwarch-
And't tomcats gone stone deef.

His owd thrombooan's seen betther days,
It's like us aw, by gum.
It's owd an bent an has moor dents
Than a one-eyed jeighner's thumb.

An when Owd Thrumble drops off perch
An' thraycles off Up Yonder,
He'll tek 'is owd thrombooan wi him-
There's nowt o' which he's fonder...

An when't Good Lord anneawnces: "Ey!
It's Judgement Day morn morn."
Owd Thrumble's Thrombooan ull caw Last Thrump
-COS IT'S LOUDER THAN GABRIEL'S 'ORN!

(These poems and more are in my Lancashire Laughter and Tears
book – available on Kindle)

About the author: A former television comedy writer, Dave Dutton is an actor specialising in quirky Northern character parts: from proper deadpan to blummin' angry and from flippin' comic to reet sad.

Along with his many other roles on British television, Dave has appeared in an incredible nine different main character parts in top British TV soap Coronation Street: from Weatherfield Gazette photographer Harry Benson to Bert Latham - barmy friend of Jack Duckworth with whom he once led a memorable fox hunt episode in the middle of the famous street with his dog Boomer.

He has also had four different roles in Emmerdale.

He plays disgraced Northern ventriloquist Bonjour Hellfire, co-starring alongside the legendary Rik Mayall in the audio series The Last Hurrah.

His latest Corrie incarnation was the feisty Kung Fu Clifford, karate expert and nosy neighbour who discovered Joy Fishwick's body after karate kicking down the door.. Before that he played Gerald Unwin, who liked a drink and a smoke and was the uncle of Shelley, former manager of the Rovers Return.

As the unscrupulous Harry Benson, the roguish Weatherfield Gazette photographer, he chained one of the unfortunate Battersby girls to a tree and took glamour shots of her ("for the lads in the darkroom"!) Along with his reporter Duncan Stott, he ruined the church wedding of Roy and Hayley.

He first came to public recognition when he appeared in several series of the big hit series Watching, set on Merseyside and the Wirral - where he brought his dead-pan humour to great effect as Oswald, the off-beat cafe owner, in this top of the ratings Granada TV situation comedy. Sky TV have reprised the series on Granada Plus many times.

He was also in the "Night To Remember" Gala Bingo and Maltesers TV commercials in which babies play football with Maltesers - while he nicks all the ones that go in his goal!

Dave has played the Postman - Fred Leeder - in Heartbeat and been featured in award-winning drama series Cops. He has also appeared in the hit series Reckless with Robson Green and as a prison guard in the hospital drama Always and Everyone with Niamh Cusack and Martin Shaw.

In 2002, he was in the main role of Grandad Pete Clulow in the Channel Four school drama and educational series for children "Looking After the Penneys" produced by Libra Television and later in the year as shopkeeper Bob Southall in BBC's police drama series Merseybeat.

In 2003 he played Ufologist Mr Skip in 6 episodes of Emmerdale; a Security Man in Granada TV's comedy series Stan the Man and the Greengrocer in YTV's new Heartbeat hospital spin-off series The Royal .In 2004, he returned to Heartbeat and also played Arthur Digweed in the comedy series 'Dead Man Weds starring Johnny Vegas and Dave Spikey.

In 2005, he appeared as cancer sufferer Neville Tweedy in several episodes of the BBC hit drama "Cutting It" (getting the chance to sing Puff the Magic Dragon at a funeral!) and also in the Gala Bingo TV ad.

In 2007, he played John Langdale in the BBC's New Street Law and also had a song he wrote called Bless Your Whiskers, Father Christmas released as a single by top Northern folk band The Houghton Weavers. Available on iTunes. He also appeared as Eric the Postman in Emmerdale.

In 2008 he returned to Emmerdale for his fourth role in the series - this time as a shopkeeper and also as Sidney Rawton in The Royal Today as well as the talent show compere in My Spy Family.

In 2011, back in Corrie as "Kung Fu Cliff" - nosy neighbour and karate expert. Farmer in Hovis ad and voiceover for Volkswagen Commercial. Headmaster in 90 minute tv production Just Henry.

Dave's books on Amazon Kindle include Lanky Panky!; Lancashire Laughter and Tears; the Book of Famous Oddballs; Horrors! And How to Be a Crafty Cruiser. Just search on Amazon or Google for further details.

Testimonials.

'Mr Dutton's mordant wit is a good match for his subject matter.'- The Guardian

'If I made awards, my trophy for the funniest book of the year would go to LANKY SPOKEN HERE!- Northants Evening Telegraph

'A really entertaining book. An accurate guide to speaking gradely proper.' - Bolton Evening News

'A witty and often hilarious read . . . a genuinely instructive manual for bewildered foreigners.' - Manchester Evening News

'The fertile phraseology makes this book a little gem, with some glittering jewels of dialect as rich and ripe as black peas, bread pudding and cow-heel pie.' Lancashire Evening Post and Chronicle

'Lanky must be saved - and Dave Dutton does much to help the cause with this book.' -Coventry Evening Telegraph

'Dave Dutton writes with all the authority of one with an ear close to the tap room. . . A light hearted collection in which the beerily bawdy jostles for attention with the near-poetic.' - Lancashire Life

'Eee, it's a lowf innit!'- A Lancashire lad
####

8574416R00035

Printed in Great Britain
by Amazon.co.uk, Ltd.,
Marston Gate.